Original title:
Sonnets Among the Stars

Copyright © 2025 Creative Arts Management OÜ
All rights reserved.

Author: Liam Sterling
ISBN HARDBACK: 978-1-80567-773-4
ISBN PAPERBACK: 978-1-80567-894-6

Phases of the Celestial Moon

In the night sky, a big round cheese,
Glowing bright, it aims to please.
Luna giggles in a crescent grin,
Hiding shyly, where to begin?

When full, she dances all around,
But waxes thick, she'll tumble down.
A lunar party with stars in tow,
Jumping craters in a cosmic show.

Gibbous moon, with a cheeky wink,
Spinning tales, making folks think.
If gravity could giggle too,
It'd bounce along, just like the dew.

As she wanes, the jokes grow stale,
Wishing she could spin a tale.
But every month, she'll rise and fall,
A jester bright, to entertain all!

Navigating the Night

In a spaceship made of cheese,
I drift past Jupiter with ease.
My GPS, a squirrel named Lou,
Keeps yelling, 'Left at the big blue.'

Stars giggle as they twinkle bright,
While Martians dance, what a sight!
I ponder over cosmic fries,
With ketchup from a comet's rise.

Eclipses of Inspiration

An eclipse pops like a surprise,
As quirky thoughts dance in the skies.
I jot them down on paper moons,
While Saturn hums its funny tunes.

The sun sneezes, a solar flare,
And planets waltz without a care.
With hiccups from the Milky Way,
I laugh at how the comets play.

Rhymes from a Distant World

On Pluto, poets wear pink hats,
And draft their lines with cosmic cats.
They write of jellybeans and cheese,
Their verses swirling with cosmic breeze.

Each rhyme goes up, then plops back down,
As aliens giggle, donning crowns.
A dance of words, a sight so rare,
With laughter echoing everywhere.

Oasis of Celestial Sights

In an oasis of starry fun,
I sip some cosmic, fizzy sun.
The planets play a game of chase,
While UFOs zoom at a dizzy pace.

A comet slides down a cosmic slide,
While space whales frolic, full of pride.
Here laughter echoes in the void,
A universe where joy's deployed.

Skies of Poetics

In the sky, a poet's dream,
Stars are laughing, or so it seems.
Writing jokes on cosmic scrolls,
While comets dance with silly goals.

They scribble rhymes on Saturn's rings,
With cosmic pens that shoot out springs.
The Milky Way spills ink so bright,
As moonbeams giggle through the night.

Twilight Verses

Twilight whispers, what a sight,
A firefly winks, "You write or bite?"
Underneath the glowing show,
Even crickets join the flow.

With stars in jars, a glowworm tale,
They sing of cows that dance and sail.
A punchline flies on a shooting star,
That's comedy from afar!

Reflecting in Celestial Waters

In puddles deep, reflections play,
The moon says, "Hey, let's rhyme today!"
Water ripples, a laughter bloom,
As stars dip in this cosmic room.

Aligned in rows like quirky ducks,
The planets spin, throwing cosmic bucks.
A starfish giggles, makes a wish,
For moon pies and a comet dish.

The Poetry of Planets

Planets swirl in a playful dance,
Mars winks at Venus, "Take a chance!"
With rhymes that float our way up high,
Even Jupiter can't help but try.

Uranus tells tales of galactic fun,
While Saturn's rings make everyone run.
They craft a verse, a twinkling cheer,
In this cosmic circus, oh dear, oh dear!

Lyrical Echoes of the Universe

In space, I lost my favorite shoe,
It floated past, oh what a view.
A comet winked and said with glee,
'That's just a fashion choice, you'll see!'

Asteroids dance in wild routines,
While Saturn spins in polka-dots, it seems.
I asked a star to join the fun,
It twinkled bright, 'I'm on the run!'

Harmonies of the Heavens

The planets gather for a jam,
Some play guitar, others a slam.
Uranus strums a cheerful tune,
While Venus croons beneath the moon.

Jupiter's rhythm shakes the night,
With meteors jumping, what a sight!
Mars drops beats with a heavy flair,
While Mercury's quick, zipping here and there.

Beyond the Twilight

The twilight laughs, a cosmic jest,
Stars gather round for a nightly fest.
Robots spin in a zero-grav,
While galaxies giggle, what a laugh!

A black hole yawns, it's time to snack,
Swallowing comets, never looking back.
With each crunch, it makes a sound,
A cosmic crunch that shakes the ground.

The Grammar of the Stars

In the grammar of the night sky,
Punctuation marks whoosh and fly.
Comets are exclamation marks, oh dear,
While periods twinkle, ever so near.

Astrological nouns float around,
Verbs make the cosmos dance and bound.
Adjectives glow bright, full of flair,
While conjunctions link the stars with care.

Dreaming with Supernovae

In the night, a star sneezed bright,
Cosmic dust turned to dazzling light.
Aliens danced, what a funny sight,
While comets giggled, taking flight.

Galaxies spun in a jovial race,
Planets tripped in an endless chase.
Black holes winked with a cheeky face,
In this universe, it's all a grace.

Starlit Epiphanies

Under the moon, a cow jumps high,
Shooting stars laugh as they pass by.
A jellyfish floats in the night sky,
Telling secrets to clouds nearby.

Saturn wears rings made of cheesy snacks,
While Pluto grumbles, it's lost its tracks.
A wink from Mars as it relaxes,
In cosmic humor, the universe cracks.

Whispered Wishes in the Cosmos

Stars twinkle, whispering their lore,
A meteor showers wishes galore.
Galactic pirates, forevermore,
Steal light from stars, always wanting more.

The moon's a pie in a cosmic bake,
Planets giggle with every quake.
They laugh together, for heaven's sake,
Creating joy with every move they make.

Ballads of the Celestial Sphere

The sun tells jokes, bright rays aglow,
While Venus prances in a celestial show.
With a wink, Mars gives a friendly blow,
As Neptune chuckles, down below.

Stardust gathers, crafting silly hats,
While comets chase their space-time rats.
In the vastness, the universe chats,
With laughter echoing in cosmic sprats.

Moonlit Melodies

Under the moon's bright, silly grin,
Crickets join in, let the fun begin.
Jupiter's waltz, a dance so light,
While owls hoot jokes that take flight.

Stars try to rhyme, a cosmic jest,
Shining so bright, they think they're the best.
But with every twinkle, their lyrics are weak,
It's laughter we seek, not a musical peak.

Stardust Scribbles

In the canvas of night, a doodle appears,
Comets that giggle, as laughter steers.
Stars write their notes with a shaky hand,
Creating a symphony that's goofy and grand.

Meteor showers, a splash of cheer,
Wishes are whispered, but none are sincere.
Planets play poker, and Saturn's won big,
While Venus just blushes, doing a jig.

Cosmic Cadence

Floating through space with a quirky beat,
Aliens dance with two left feet.
The sun strums a tune, quite out of key,
While asteroids roll, as happy as can be.

Galaxies twirl in a cosmic ball,
Gravity's strong, but not for them all.
When laughter erupts from a supernova's flare,
Stars chuckle lightly, floating in air.

Ethereal Echoes

Echoes of laughter bounce off the night,
As space cats frolic, an amusing sight.
Nebulas tease with colors so bold,
Making ticklish sounds like stories retold.

Black holes play hide and seek, what a game!
Planetary pals shout out, "Hey, we're not lame!"
Each cosmic giggle a astrophysical tease,
In the universe's party, it's sure to please.

Rhymes of the Nebula

In the sky, the stars wear shoes,
Dancing swiftly, they've got the moves.
One tripped over a comet's tail,
Laughed so hard, it began to wail.

A quasar quipped, 'I'm the brightest!'
While black holes claimed, 'We're the slightest!'
They joined a game of cosmic tag,
But who will ever catch that snag?

Elegies Beyond the Horizon

The moon declared a pizza night,
With toppings made of stardust light.
They called the sun to bring the cheese,
But he just burned them all with ease!

Jupiter joined with gas and flair,
Said, 'I baked cookies; can I share?'
But Martians came with olives grim,
And turned that treat into a whim!

Starlit Soliloquy

A shooting star wrote poems fast,
But they all seemed to end up lashed.
Venus chuckled, 'What a mess!'
While Mercury thought, 'I must confess!'

Each verse just slipped like solar flares,
Falling neatly through space affairs.
Yet in the end, they had their fun,
Creating chaos, one by one!

Verses in the Void

In the cosmos, a cat named Star,
Said, 'I'll be a pop star, how bizarre!'
With a laser pen, he drew the crowds,
But forgot his lyrics—how loud he prowled!

He sang of planets, black and round,
But they all rolled away, no sound.
Yet in that void, he found a tune,
And danced with comets under the moon!

Celestial Verses Whispered at Dawn

In morning's glow, the giggles rise,
As planets tease with winking eyes.
The sun pours laughter, bright and bold,
While space cats pounce on beams of gold.

A comet tail, a slick banana,
And meteors dance the Cha-Cha-Cha.
Jupiter's jokes, they fly so high,
While cosmic dust does tickle the sky.

Stars hold hands, they spin and twirl,
Creating a cosmic, giddy whirl.
Nebulas wink with playful glee,
As the universe sings: "Come dance with me!"

Starlit Rhapsody of Heartstrings

Under stardust, hearts collide,
With twinkling lights, we laugh, we bide.
Venus winks, like a cheeky friend,
While Saturn laughs from around the bend.

Love rockets flame in giggly flight,
As Cupid's arrow takes a bite.
In laughter's orbit, we float around,
With love notes drifting, cosmic bound.

Hearts in motion, like meteor showers,
With hugs that bloom like cosmic flowers.
The Milky Way hums a silly tune,
While planets prance beneath the moon.

Twilight's Illumination in Verse

As twilight paints with purple hues,
The cosmic giggle stirs the blues.
Constellations make sideways grins,
While galaxies wink, where fun begins.

The moon dons shades; a rockstar's flair,
While space mice play without a care.
Jokes float gently on solar breeze,
As time forgets to bend the knees.

Pulsars thump with a bouncy bass,
While dark matter does a goofy chase.
Twinkling laughter fills the night,
In the cosmic dance, all feel just right.

Cosmic Lines of Love and Longing

In the great abyss, my heart does yawn,
As stars ride bikes 'til the break of dawn.
With every spark, a dream takes flight,
And aliens dance in the pale moonlight.

Love letters written in cosmic dust,
Float on the breeze; it's all a must.
With black holes laughing at silly things,
As comets zip by on shiny wings.

Our hearts are planets in joyful chase,
In this vast universe, we find our place.
Galaxies spin with whimsical cheer,
As we giggle together, year after year.

Illuminated Echoes

In dim-lit rooms where echoes play,
The shadows dance and sway away.
A cat with dreams takes starry leaps,
While humans snooze and count their sheep.

A comet zooms past with a grin,
It tickles horns of a cosmic kin.
With laughter spun from diamond dust,
We chase our thoughts, in stardust, trust.

Chasing the Stellar Muse

A little star with sparkly shoes,
Danced through the night with cosmic blues.
It tripped on beams of moonlight yarn,
And fell right into a sitting barn.

In every corner, laughs do play,
As cows debate the Milky Way.
They moo their dreams beneath the sky,
While meteors flirt and wink nearby.

Twilight Narratives

The twilight sings with silly tunes,
As squirrels wear hats and groove with loons.
They strut around in fancy gear,
Chasing fireflies not far, but near.

A fox recites his love in rhyme,
To a starling that's quite out of time.
Together they twirl in endless glee,
While crickets play on, oh so free!

Narratives of the Night

The night rolls in with jokes galore,
While owls hoot loud, begging for more.
A raccoon dons a mask so sly,
While stars paint patterns in the sky.

The moon just chuckles, round and bright,
As shadows prance left and right.
In this grand tale, the laughter flows,
As creatures giggle under glows.

Chasing Constellations

In the sky, I see a moose,
With antlers made of shining juice.
He hops from star to star so bright,
Sipping starlight every night.

A comet flies with candy bars,
While planets dance in silly cars.
They giggle, twirl, and spin around,
In this cosmic playground, joy is found.

The Milky Way is made of cream,
I float on it, a frothy dream.
With chocolate sprinkles made of light,
I feast on sweets until it's bright.

As I chase these dazzling sights,
I lose my shoes on cosmic nights.
The universe, a wacky show,
With laughter echoing as I go.

Lyrical Luminaries

The stars sing songs of silly tunes,
While planets strut in feathered plumes.
An asteroid trips, and down it goes,
Laughing with a cosmic nose.

Each moonbeam winks with playful glee,
Tickling the vastness of the sea.
A starry choir starts to hum,
As comets come, and drum and drum.

Neptune wears a tutu, oh so bright,
While Jupiter juggles all in sight.
With cosmic giggles floating near,
Every twinkle beams with cheer.

In the cosmos' grand ballet,
Lyrical lights come out to play.
With a wink and twist, they twist and spin,
Creating laughter where they've been.

The Language of Light

In whispers soft, the starlight speaks,
Of cosmic jokes and funny weeks.
Galactic giggles fill the air,
As light beams bounce without a care.

A supernova bursts with flair,
Confetti glitters everywhere.
Each photon teases with a grin,
Inviting others to spin and spin.

The sun, a fiery joker bold,
Tells tales of time, both new and old.
While meteors wish upon their fate,
And twinkle back before it's late.

In this language, laughter flies,
From star to star, a grand surprise.
The secrets of the night, we share,
In twinkling lights beyond compare.

Galaxies in Stanza

My telescope, a magic wand,
Shows galaxies as a playful pond.
They splash and play with cosmic zest,
In a starlit game, they jest and jest.

Each black hole wears a silly hat,
While Martians dance with a chubby cat.
In swirling arms, they skip and prance,
Inviting all to join the dance.

Shooting stars hold a party bright,
With wishes tossed in sheer delight.
While gravity laughs, "Come take a ride!"
On this wild rocket, we'll glide and glide.

So grab your friends and join the fun,
For galaxies shine like they've just won.
With every verse, the cosmos glows,
In this universe where laughter flows.

Dreams Weave Through Celestial Canopies

In the night, the owls gossip near,
While roosters dance with a cosmic cheer.
Stars wear pajamas, all cozy and bright,
As planets play tag in the velvet night.

Moonbeams giggle, casting shadows large,
While comets race by, each one a charge.
Alien llamas are prancing about,
As cosmic confetti rains down with a shout.

Celestial popcorn, we munch with delight,
As meteors dive, what a silly sight!
Galaxies swirl, in this party we throw,
The universe chuckles, come join in the show.

So let's sip stardust, let's laugh and spin,
While black holes joke, "It's a riot within!"
With dreams and quirks, we float here and there,
In this cosmic wonder, with plenty to share.

Echoes of Celestial Love Songs

The sun serenades, with tunes oh so clear,
While asteroids fashion their love songs sincere.
Jupiter winks with romantic delight,
As Venus giggles, her dress shining bright.

Stars twirl in pairs, a dance of romance,
While Milky Way twinkles, urging the chance.
A comet proposes, it's a sight to behold,
With a ring made of rocks and a story retold.

Neptune laments, a tear in his eye,
While Saturn's rings shine, oh me, oh my!
The universe sighs, lovesick and true,
In the cosmic ballad, it's just me and you.

With echoes of laughter, love fills the space,
As we chase the starlight, a twinkling embrace.
Through photons and giggles, we frolic along,
In this playful ballet, where all love belongs.

Fragments of Light in the Cosmic Tapestry

Dust bunnies dance in the Milky Way seam,
While light beams bounce, like a cosmic dream.
Black holes hiccup, their belly's a whirl,
As quasars laugh bright, adding sparkle and twirl.

Alien squirrels juggle stars in the night,
While rockets play hopscotch in cheerful flight.
The universe giggles, with a wink and a spin,
As constellations argue, "Where do we begin?"

Supernovas spark, like fireworks in cheer,
While time's just a fable, let's drink it in beer.
Fragments of laughter, stitched in the sky,
In this silly tapestry, we twinkle and fly.

With whispers of stardust, we giggle and weave,
Creating a saga, we won't dare believe.
In this grand cosmic quilt, we find our delight,
In fragments of joy, wrapped snugly at night.

Poetic Reflections in the Starlight

A shooting star trips, oh what fun!
While planets play peek-a-boo, one by one.
Galactic giggles echo in the air,
As starlight tickles without a care.

Moonlight dons shades, all stylish and cool,
As comets become jesters, a cosmic fool.
Black holes share secrets, the comical kind,
While gravity chuckles, "You're all so blind!"

We toast with stardust, our cups overflow,
With laughter and light in this grand cosmic show.
The universe sparkles in brilliant delight,
As we swap silly jokes in the warm starlight.

With poetic musings, we frolic and prance,
As nebulas twirl in a joyous dance.
In reflections of humor, we twinkle and beam,
In this whimsical cosmos, we're living the dream.

The Dance of Words in Galactic Harmony

In a bar of cosmic light, they twirl,
Nouns and verbs in a cosmic whirl.
Adjectives dressed in sparkly threads,
While silly adverbs bounce on their heads.

Planets giggle as syntax plays,
Commas dance in a funky phase.
With every line, laughter erupts,
In galactic tomfoolery, all are cupped.

Stars trade puns in a radiant jest,
While meteors join the lively fest.
Rhymes of laughter fill the night,
In this stellar dance, pure delight!

Beyond the Horizon of Emotion

A poet's heart works overtime,
With jokes wrapped in celestial rhyme.
Emotions float in zero-G,
As laughter rings from sea to sea.

Shooting stars chuckle with delight,
At feelings far too complex to write.
The joy of words is pure and bright,
Like pizza delivered in the night.

So let your heart take silly flight,
Over galaxies of sheer delight.
For in this cosmic canvas spread,
We paint with laughter instead of dread.

Ethereal Odes Beneath the Aurora

Under auroras, quirkiness thrives,
Where poets craft with vibrant jives.
Verses leap like funny socks,
As emotions tickle like paradox clocks.

In the shimmer of lights, we scribble fast,
Rhymes that ripple, and humor amassed.
Words dance wildly, a carnival scene,
A mishmash of whimsy, oh so keen!

Giggles rustle in the northern skies,
While metaphors throw glowing pies.
With laughter echoing through the night,
We find our joy within the flight.

Heartfelt Stanzas Lost in the Cosmos

Floating verses in cosmic seas,
With punchlines riding on solar breeze.
Stanzas laugh as they bounce around,
In this vastness, joy is profound.

Comets chuckle, with tails aflame,
As love and humor poke the same.
Each heartfelt word, a playful tease,
Like space-sized bubbles that never freeze.

So join the fun in this astral dance,
Where feelings swirl and thoughts prance.
In the cosmos' hug, we find our place,
With laughter echoing, we embrace!

Illuminated Dreams

In slumber deep, my thoughts take flight,
A grand balloon, lost in the night.
I chase the comets, bright and bold,
But trip on space debris, uncontrolled.

The aliens dance in their funky suits,
With disco balls and jellyfruit roots.
They invite me over for a space tea,
But I spill it all, oh woe is me!

With rocket skates, I zoom and glide,
Through moons made of cheese, I slip and slide.
I giggle with stars, we laugh and prance,
Unruly space jesters in a cosmic dance.

As the dreams fade, the night turns to morn,
I wake up grinning, my heart still torn.
Was it just a dream, all that delight?
Or a funny trip through the cosmic night?

Verses of the Cosmic Tide

The waves of space crash with a giggle,
As cosmic surfers ride and wiggle.
The planets clap in rhythmic cheers,
While aliens hum and share their beers.

A giant octopus flips a rhyme,
In verses that stretch through space and time.
It juggles moons like bouncing balls,
While echoing laughter through cosmic halls.

On asteroids, we have our fun,
Gazing at galaxies, then off we run.
Each star a wink, each comet a joke,
As laughter spreads, our cosmic cloak.

When the tide pulls back, we wave goodbye,
To the space-time circus in the sky.
With silly thoughts from a starry spree,
I ponder if the stars are laughing at me!

Celestial Serenade

Under a sunbeam, I find a stage,
With shooting stars and a moon-lit page.
The galaxies twirl in a joyful dance,
As I recite lines that make them prance.

A chorus of crickets strum their strings,
While Saturn giggles, and laughter rings.
The sun rolls its eyes, a cosmic sight,
As I trip over stardust, what a fright!

With twinkling lights as my backup band,
We jam in harmony, just as we planned.
But the black hole swallows a note or two,
And we burst out laughing; what else can you do?

So under the skies, I take a bow,
To the crowd of stars, I thank them now.
For cosmic melodies in a whimsical spree,
Have turned my serenade to pure glee!

Poetry in the Firmament

The universe whispers a quirky line,
About a space cat who drinks moonshine.
With whiskers that sparkle, eyes like the sun,
She plays with her yarn, what cosmic fun!

The meteors dash in a slapstick race,
While planets roll their eyes at the ridiculous chase.
I scribble the folly in a floating book,
As aliens peek, all friendly, they look.

In a nebula filled with cosmic pies,
I feast on a slice blessed by starlit skies.
Each bite brings laughter, each crumb a delight,
In the poetry of dusk, we all unite.

As the firmament yawns, bidding adieu,
The laughter echoes, forever anew.
With silly tales spun in the starlit dome,
Every night is a verse, my celestial home!

The Infinity of Thoughts in Orbit

In orbits wide, our thoughts do spin,
They loop and whirl, where do we begin?
A cosmic joke, it seems we're lost,
With each new thought, we count the cost.

The planets laugh, they wink and tease,
While we debate the meaning of cheese.
Galaxies chat, they share their dreams,
Spinning tales in whimsical teams.

What if the stars just want a dance?
To sway and twirl, not leave to chance.
They giggle softly, a twinkling fun,
As we scribble notes, aiming for the sun.

So here we are, a gaggle of brains,
Orbiting thoughts, like love-struck trains.
In the infinity of our silly plight,
We find our joy in the cosmic light.

Chasing Comets with Words

I wrote a poem for a comet's tail,
It zoomed by fast, but left a trail.
With every word, I tried to catch,
The fleeting spark, an elusive match.

Oh, comet dear, please slow your glow,
I need more time for my genius flow.
Yet off you dart, in a brilliant burst,
Leaving my verses just slightly cursed.

I toss my words into the dark,
Hoping they'll light up with a spark.
But all I get are silence and crickets,
As I hunt for Sunday's cosmic tickets.

Let's race through space on a rhyming spree,
With comet tails as our poetry.
We'll chase them down, like kids on bikes,
Creating laughter amongst the spikes.

Harmonies Composed on Celestial Shores

On shores of stars, we build our sand,
A symphony crafted by a silly hand.
With plucked guitar strings made of light,
We strum the night, it feels so right.

The waves of comets crash and hum,
As we compose this nightly drum.
With dancing moons as our back-up band,
We're tuning giggles, isn't it grand?

We harmonize with talking rocks,
That gossip loud in cosmic socks.
The constellations clap their hands,
As we create our vibrant strands.

So here we sing, off beats, a thrill,
On celestial shores, we chase the quill.
Our song of stars, both funny and bright,
Leaves echoes of laughter lingering in flight.

A Symphony of Celestial Whispers

In quiet tones, the stars confide,
Whispers float through the cosmic ride.
They snicker softly behind our backs,
As we misstep in our starlit tracks.

Oh, listen close, the comets will sing,
About the antics of our earthly bling.
They tease the planets for their silly hats,
While we search for love in dated chats.

Each twinkle tells of a joke unknown,
Of all the seeds of laughter sown.
So grab a chair, let's sit and see,
What cosmic giggles await from thee.

Their symphony swells, a joyful sound,
In the galaxy where fun is found.
With every whisper, we join the jest,
In a universe filled with humor blessed.

Luminous Lines

In the sky, lights dance and prance,
A cosmic ball of happenstance.
Why do aliens wear such bright shoes?
Maybe they're just out to amuse!

Comets with hairdos, quite absurd,
Stars gossip, but they're hard to hear.
Jupiter snickers at Earth's plight,
While Venus competes in a fashion fight.

Planets twirl in a celestial spree,
Saturn's rings, a blinged-out decree.
Astronauts float, pretending to glue,
Their helmets stuck—oh what a view!

Echoes in the Ether

In the void, echoes sing in jest,
Black holes play hide and seek, no rest.
Mars insists it's the red of passion,
While aliens giggle, lacking compassion.

Constellations spell out silly names,
Like 'Pizza Star,' playing wild games.
The Moon rolls its eyes at Earth's fuss,
While the Sun just laughs, "Don't bother us!"

Orbs in orbit, a comical fright,
Ceres forgot to wear its nightlight.
Stars drop by for a friendly tease,
In the cosmos, it's all just a breeze!

Rhythms of the Night Sky

Dancing planets in a jolly show,
While meteorites put on a faux glow.
Orion's belt, the latest bling,
Stars twirl and spin—a cosmic swing!

A telescope spies a Martian prank,
Uranus giggles from its blank flank.
Stardust confetti rains down on Earth,
As aliens declare a day of mirth.

Galaxies whirl in wild delight,
Creating worlds in the deep night.
Stars trade secrets, a giggling spree,
In this whimsical vastness, we all feel free!

Galactic Ballads

In the night, a choir of stars sings,
They argue over who wears the blings.
Supernova shouts, "Look at me shine!"
While Saturn's rings glow, "That's just fine!"

On Pluto, a party, but it's quite chill,
The planets show up, just for the thrill.
Neptune's high notes cause laughter galore,
As cosmic beings race for the door.

Asteroids roll like unruly teens,
While cosmic dust floats in bubbly scenes.
The universe chuckles, full of glee,
In this grand ballad, we're all so free!

Dreamscapes Danced in Moonlight

In dreams, the cows wear shoes so bright,
Upon the moon, they dance at night.
The cheese they chase, a dream so wild,
Who would have thought? That cow is styled!

A hedgehog flies a kite with flair,
While squirrels juggle nuts in the air.
The stars giggle, twinkling wide,
As rabbits hop on eagles' ride.

The clouds, they giggle in delight,
As rabbits dress in suits so tight.
With marshmallow dreams, they bounce and sway,
In moonlit realms, they laugh and play.

The owl wears glasses, wise and neat,
As fireflies dance on tiny feet.
In this soft glow, no worries exist,
Just lighthearted laughs and nature's twist.

Lyrical Orbits of the Soul

In cosmic realms, the llamas sing,
They float through space on a gelatin wing.
With bubblewrap on their feet to dance,
Each track leads into a lunar prance.

The sun winks down, a mischievous flame,
While planets play an interstellar game.
Each star wears a funny hat and bow,
As meteors flash by with a giggling wow.

A comet sneezes, spreading glittery dust,
The universe spins, with chaos, it must!
Celestial jokes ripple through the night,
As laughter rings and fills the starlit sight.

With cosmic cookies baked from the moon,
The astronauts dance to a whimsical tune.
And while gravity fails to hold them tight,
They float and twirl, what a comical sight!

Echoes of Eternity in Ink

In scribbles found on parchment old,
The wizards tell of tales bold.
A dragon wearing polka dot pants,
Performs on stage with fanciful dance.

A quill that hops on tiny feet,
Jots down tales of a pig's grand feat.
As unicorns giggle and tease the air,
Writing worlds filled with whimsical flair.

The verses twist like vines in trees,
A tortoise wins, about which all freeze.
With ink that glows as interesting lore,
Every line brings laughter, tempting more.

In the margins, caricatures play,
As gnomes recount adventures of the day.
Each echo lingers, light and spry,
As pens sparkle and spirits fly.

Celestial Musings Under the Night Sky

Beneath the twinkle of stars so bright,
A cat dons pajamas, a comical sight.
With a telescope made of macaroni,
She charts the skies like a cheerful phony.

The moon, a giant, with a cheerful grin,
Hosts a tea party, where all join in.
Mars brings cookies, a tale to share,
While Venus wears a feathered chair.

Jokes shoot like meteors, wild and free,
As cosmic clowns laugh in harmony.
Galaxies spin, each twist and twirl,
While stars play tag, in this dreamy whirl.

Constellations giggle and intertwine,
A jester's dance along the divine.
And when the dawn cracks the night in half,
The cosmos smiles, oh, what a laugh!

Celestial Cadences

In the sky, a bright balloon,
Floats past the Milky Way's tune.
Stars giggle as comets whiz,
Chasing dreams, oh what a fizz!

Jupiter dances with a twinkling grin,
While Mars plays hide and seek again.
Venus wears a sparkly crown,
Orbiting with a silly frown.

Galaxy pets wag their tails,
Barking at the cosmic trails.
Nebulas swirl with colors bold,
As they tell jokes that never get old.

Asteroids form a wacky band,
Singing tunes across the land.
Galactic giggles fill the night,
As stars wink with pure delight.

Rhymes of Radiant Realms

In a realm where planets laugh,
Saturn's rings made a silly gaff.
Uranus rolled and fell on cue,
Spinning jokes that were quite askew.

Neptune wears a fluffy hat,
While Pluto plays the role of chat.
Cosmic critters dance and sway,
Underneath the Milky Way.

Constellations throw a ball,
Orion trips, oh what a fall!
Twirling stars in a wobbly spin,
As they bask in laughter's din.

Zany meteors whiz on past,
Racing each other, oh what a blast!
They all giggle at the sound,
Of cosmic humor all around.

Etched in the Ether

Floating dreams in the darkest night,
Stars are plotting a funny flight.
With winks and laughs they collide,
Twirling comets as they glide.

Echoes of giggles across the void,
In the cosmos where fun is enjoyed.
Moons make faces, oh so bright,
As they joke with all their might.

An alien chef with starry fries,
Serving up laughter in the skies.
Galaxies hum a merry tune,
Under the eye of a cheerful moon.

Celestial whispers hear the call,
Of silly jokes that tickle us all.
In this space of joy and cheer,
Every giggle rings loud and clear.

Muses of the Night

Tiny planets with jokes to share,
Wobbling through the moonlit air.
Shooting stars race by with glee,
Saying, "Catch us if you can, you see!"

Constellations form a line,
Waiting for their chance to shine.
Sirius grinned, a corny star,
Telling tales from near and far.

A cosmic wink from the Venusian crew,
As they dance with a bright blue hue.
Galactic giggles spread like light,
While comets laugh through endless night.

In a universe with playful souls,
Every twinkle and blink consoles.
So here's to laughter shining wide,
With every star, joy takes a ride.

Echoes of a Cosmic Dance

In space, we twirl like clumsy clowns,
With planets laughing, spinning 'round.
An asteroid trips, and off it goes,
While comets wink with silly shows.

Gravity plays its mischievous tricks,
As moons pull pranks, they're quite the mix.
A dance-off in the Milky Way,
Where aliens join and sway all day.

Black holes giggle, with a whoosh so loud,
As meteors dive, bursting through the crowd.
The stars light up, with twinkling grins,
In this cosmic ballet, everyone spins.

So if you peek into the night sky,
Remember the laughter that floats on high.
For every twinkle, a giggle's found,
In this giant circus, where joy's unbound.

Luminous Traces of Time

Once, a star typed with a cosmic pen,
Wrote jokes for black holes, again and again.
As time flew by, they laughed and winked,
At all the silly things they'd linked.

Nebulas blush in colors so bright,
While planets gossip about their night flight.
The sun tells stories of days long past,
While comets burst forth, leaving trails so fast.

Galaxies giggle in spiraled embrace,
Poking fun at planets stuck in their place.
A supernova did a dance with flare,
Lighting the cosmos with a flair most rare.

So travel through ages with laughter in mind,
Where time's just a joke that we've all designed.
In this radiant realm, humor's the key,
Unlocking the wonders for you and me.

Fireflies in the Galaxy

Tiny sparks swarm like buzzing flies,
In the vastness of night, they meet with surprise.
They flash and they flicker, a cosmic delight,
Chasing each other through the starry night.

When meteors race in a glorious dash,
Funny faces form in a glowing flash.
They wink at the moons, who clumsily shine,
Swaying to rhythms that feel quite divine.

A firefly giggles, spinning in place,
While satellites play, with smiles on their face.
In this glowing ballroom that never gets old,
The universe dances, in stories retold.

So join in the fun, let your worries take flight,
Embrace the odd beauty of the infinite night.
For in this grand party, we're all a part,
As fireflies twinkle and dance from the heart.

Whispers in the Celestial Breeze

Galaxies whisper, secrets galore,
In a breeze made of laughter, forever to soar.
Stars poke fun at our Earthly ways,
As they twinkle and chuckle on endless displays.

Supernova sings a silly old tune,
While asteroids dance like they're late for a noon.
Each solar wind carries a message of glee,
A reminder that joy is universal, you see.

With meteors zipping and comets that dive,
The cosmos engages in a playful jive.
A cosmic ballet of laughter and sound,
Where the echoes of joy can be truly found.

So when you gaze at the night sky above,
Remember the wonders that dance with love.
For even in silence, the universe speaks,
In the whispers of laughter that time gently leaks.

Twilight Ink

In twilight's haze, the ink does dance,
A wobbly comet, given the chance.
It writes of ducks and silly moons,
And space-time's funny, silly tunes.

With each great stroke, it spills a thought,
Of how the stars are often caught.
In laughter bright, they twist and twirl,
A cosmic joke in a dazzling swirl.

The planets giggle as they collide,
In irony, their orbits bide.
While asteroids keep tripping by,
And we just watch, with an amused sigh.

So let your pen drip starlit cheer,
In cosmic humor, let's all steer.
For in the night, with ink in hand,
We craft a world, both bright and grand.

Threads of the Universe

Threads woven tight in cosmic spins,
Laughing at all our little sins.
Stitching together stars so bold,
To keep warm the stories told.

A yarn about a moonlit cat,
Who juggles planets just for that.
With every throw, a solar flare,
And nearby stars just stop and stare.

Galaxies crack up, they can't contain,
The game of twinkle, it's all the same.
As comets chuckle on their flight,
Across the vast, bewildering night.

So weave your dreams on this thread of space,
With laughter bright, let joy embrace.
For in the fabric of the sky,
We find our fun, where all can fly.

Verses Drift in the Nebula

In a nebula, where giggles float,
Verses sail like a rickety boat.
They bump and crash, but never fall,
Through cosmic fog, they loop and sprawl.

A star once said, 'That's quite a rhyme,
But please refrain from using mime!'
And just like that, the silence broke,
As laughter spilled with every poke.

Supernova laughs, exploding bright,
Echoes of humor throughout the night.
Stars with bodies, oh what a sight,
They dance like children, pure delight.

So drift along this playful stream,
In every verse, let laughter beam.
For in the nebula's joyful grasp,
We find our muse, in every gasp.

On the Edge of the Cosmos

On the edge where whimsies play,
Cosmic kids are in disarray.
Playing tag with shooting stars,
While giggling loud from Martian bars.

They flip and flop, break all the rules,
As Saturn spins, and whimsy fuels.
Black holes grin, with secrets in tow,
Telling tales that overflow.

The universe winks, a cheeky grin,
As mishaps happen, where to begin?
With every blunder, each twist of fate,
The cosmos chuckles, never late.

So join the fun, don't be shy,
On this edge, where dreams can fly.
In starlit laughter, let's unite,
And paint the void with pure delight.

A Journey Through the Constellation of Desire

In a galaxy where wishes play,
I stumbled on a comet's stray.
It winked and tossed its sparkling light,
I chased it through the starry night.

Neptune laughed, his rings aglow,
'These dreams are tricky; take it slow!'
A moonbeam teased, 'Come dance with me!'
We twirled through tales of cosmic glee.

Mars tossed candy from the sky,
I felt like I could almost fly.
But fell into a black hole's grin,
Now I must find a way back in!

Jupiter with his stormy stare,
Said, 'Strive, my friend, with cosmic flair!'
So here I float, with dreams held tight,
On a journey past the stars tonight.

Celestial Canvas Painted with Dreams

In a canvas where the cosmos swirls,
A painting of silly, dancing worlds.
Venus giggles under her veil,
While Saturn's rings spin like a tale.

I dipped my brush in stardust bright,
Swirled in blush of pure delight.
Orion winks with arrows aimed,
But his target? Just a dog's name!

Constellations kick in cosmic dance,
Together they frolic, given a chance.
I paint with laughter, joy and cheer,
As shooting stars bring dreams both near.

The Milky Way spills, a creamy drink,
While comets sip and stars all wink.
In this funny world where dreams collide,
I let my imagination ride.

Celestial Whispers

Beneath the night, where secrets peek,
The stars start chatting, cheek to cheek.
'Hey, did you hear what Mars just said?'
He tripped on space dust and fell in bed!

Orion rolled his eyes in jest,
'That clumsy guy, he never rests!'
While comets zoom with laughter bright,
Shooting past our giggles all night.

And Venus, oh, she's quite the tease,
Flirts with planets, does just as she pleases.
She swirls with charm, and a wink or two,
While Jupiter nods, 'I've got a few!'

In this midnight chat, no frowns in sight,
We laugh and whisper till morning light.
In cosmic realms where humor thrives,
Celestial whispers keep our dreams alive.

Verses Beneath the Milky Way

Under the blanket of twinkling gaze,
We scribble laughter in a cosmic haze.
Aliens dance, in polka-dot tights,
While shooting stars jam through the nights.

Giggles echo from asteroids near,
'I've lost my spaceship! It's in high gear!'
The sun chuckles, warm and wide,
As planets join the silly ride.

A playful breeze from the cosmic sea,
Whispers jokes of pure esprit.
'What did the black hole say to the sun?
You're pulling me in, we're destined for fun!'

And so we write these verses bright,
Laughing together, pure delight.
Beneath the Milky Way's embrace,
We craft our dreams in a shared space.

Nocturnal Reflections of Heartfelt Prose

In shadows cast by moonlight glow,
The cats play poker while we lay low.
They deal their cards with utmost flair,
As we just sit, pretending not to stare.

With twinkling eyes, they call our bluff,
But who knew felines could be so tough?
A night of laughter fills the air,
While mice arrange a grand affair.

Sneaking cheese like thieves at night,
The surprise attack brings such delight.
We cheer our pets, though they just yawn,
And dream of fish until the dawn.

In dreams we soar, so bold, so free,
As cats play kings in our reverie.
We chuckle loud, we laugh and tease,
For fun on nights like this, we seize.

Unwritten Tales in the Milky Way

Upon the starlit roof we lie,
And ponder why the squirrels fly.
Did birds slip on some cosmic goo?
Or maybe they just think it's cool?

A comet zips, a meteor flares,
It's squirrels hosting galaxy fairs.
Bouncing around on privy chairs,
While we just watch in dazed glares.

"Would you like some cheese?" one squirrel asks,
While plotting heroics in silly masks.
We sip stardust in our fizzy drinks,
And marvel at the twilight blinks.

The universe laughs with all its might,
While squirrels dance in the soft moonlight.
These tales will fade as we drift away,
Yet who knew humor ruled the Milky Way?

Poetic Constellations Guiding Hearts

Stars winked down in a cheeky way,
As we planned our picnic in bright bouquet.
They said, "Forget the rules, just have fun!"
Until ants marched in. Our food was done!

With every bite came buzzing sounds,
Our laughter echoed, bounced around.
And as we danced, they joined the line,
A parade of critters, all out to dine.

Constellations chuckled in the night,
As we shared tales that brought delight.
The sky blushed pink at our comic quests,
While Luna rolled her eyes, she was impressed.

Shooting stars would gather near,
To toss us wishes fueled by cheer.
So here's a toast to laughter's gleam,
Guided by stars, we live our dream!

Love Letters in the Nebula

A love letter reads, in cosmic ink,
"Your smile's a quasar, don't you think?"
While balloon animals float by in grace,
We write our notes in a fluffy space.

With heart-shaped asteroids all around,
And playful aliens dancing bound.
We giggle under a quilt of night,
As space dust sprinkles our love so bright.

The planets twist in a wobbly dance,
As we try to steal a fleeting glance.
"Is that a comet, or just your hair?"
Both sparkled fiercely, a cosmic pair.

So let our love be the brightest star,
With goofy humor as near as far.
We'll write our tales in nebula hues,
And send them off in interstellar blues.

Starlit Rhyme

In a galaxy far, they play a game,
With winks and giggles, they call each name.
Planets tumble, they all take a spin,
Join the ruckus, let the fun begin!

Comets race by, with tails that they flaunt,
Whispering secrets, of things that they haunt.
Neptune's got jokes, and so does the Sun,
When laughter erupts, they all join as one.

Black holes chuckle, they swallow in jest,
While asteroids play, they never can rest.
Stardust and jokes float up to the sky,
Under this shimmer, the spirits fly high.

So let's dance among, this cosmic brigade,
With giggles and laughter, that never will fade.
In this playful realm, where star friends unite,
We can't take it seriously, oh what a sight!

Cosmic Reflections

Planets peep through, their curious eyes,
Wondering who wrote those terrible rhymes.
Venus spills tea, with a grin on her face,
As Saturn just laughs, in a ringside embrace.

Asteroids bump, in a cosmic parade,
While meteors laugh, they've got jokes ready-made.
Galaxies twirl, as they dance in delight,
Falling in laughter, throughout the night.

Uranus quips, with a pun quite absurd,
While Mars rolls his eyes; it's just too unheard.
But jovial giants, with hearts big and round,
Make merry together, with joy that's profound.

So gaze up at night, with a smile on your face,
For space has its charm, and a quirky grace.
With billion-light jokes, that keep twinkling bright,
A cosmic collection of laughter and light.

Ode to the Galactic Dance

In a swirling ballet, stars twirl and swirl,
With twinkling toes in an endless whirl.
Planets groove close, with a bumbling cheer,
While black holes just hog, all the space that is near.

Jupiter winks, in his gigantic spree,
While Earth joins the fun, pouting with glee.
Mars has some moves, that just steal the show,
While moons giggle softly, putting on a glow.

Shooting stars leap, with a boisterous flair,
As cosmic confetti falls freely in air.
Each nebula shines, with a chuckle and snort,
In this whimsical realm, where the laughter is sport.

So grab your space boots, let's whirl to the beat,
In the galactic dance, life's a fun little treat.
With joy unconfined, we'll cha-cha and prance,
In this riotous ballet, come join the dance!

Celestial Sonnetry

A comet once joked with a wink and a spin,
As starlight giggled, a new game to begin.
The Milky Way chuckled, a chuckle profound,
With laughter that echoed, all around they found.

Two moons had a contest, who could shine best,
While nearby, the sun sipped his tea with a jest.
Neptune sang softly, a tune light and sweet,
As Saturn kept spinning, tapping his feet.

Constellations chuckled, with tales to unfold,
In a galaxy bright, other stories grow old.
They gathered their courage, to paint the night sky,
With silly old legends we use to get by.

So step into starlight, let humor ignite,
In this cosmic playground, all is delight.
A universe vast, where giggles take flight,
Join the celestial breeze, make your spirits bright.

Verse from the Veil of the Universe

In a cloak of night, the moon winks bright,
Stars giggle softly, what a silly sight!
Cosmic dust bunnies dance in their glee,
Even black holes chuckle, oh can't you see?

Asteroids zoom by, they dart and they dash,
While comets swoop down to join the splash.
In cosmic cafes, planets sip their brew,
The Milky Way's laughing, as she stirs her stew.

Jupiter's jokes are a roaring delight,
Mars tries stand-up but just takes flight.
Uranus snickers, "This is a blast!"
While Neptune shouts, "I'm such a gas!"

The stars are a lively, comedic crew,
With pranks and puns that are fresh and new.
In the wide expanse, where laughter's reborn,
The universe giggles from dusk until dawn.

Galaxies of Emotion Unfurled

In the dance of the cosmos, feelings collide,
Stars shed their tears, but they giggle with pride.
A supernova sneezes, exploding the night,
While Venus is blushing, a silly sight!

Saturn spins stories with rings made of gold,
Whispers of laughter from ages old.
Cosmic clowns tumble through meteors' rain,
Tickling the void, there's no room for pain.

In the laughter of comets, we find our delight,
Eclipses do cartwheels, what a joyful flight!
Astrological puns in the dust of the skies,
Like stars on a stage, with glittering eyes.

Galaxies spin tales with a humorous twang,
Through twinkling laughter, their joy's in the slang.
With winks from the heavens, how bright they will claim,

Even celestial bodies are playing the game!

Rhythms of the Infinite Cosmos

In the sway of the planets, there's a jolly beat,
Stars tap their toes, can you feel the heat?
Galaxies twirl in an interstellar ballet,
As laughter and music keep worries at bay.

The dance of the comets, a graceful cha-cha,
While nebulae giggle, "Aren't we the stars?"
In cosmic rhythms, even black holes hum,
To the tune of a universe, infinitely fun!

Quasars are crooning, with a jazz-like flair,
Singing of wonders drifting through the air.
With every beat strummed on stardust guitars,
The universe pulses, a tune sung by stars.

So waltz with the moons, and shimmy with light,
Through the twinkling wonders of the glorious night.
In the heart of it all, find the joy in the rhyme,
For laughter's the rhythm, standing the test of time.

Starlit Epistles of Desire

Written in stardust, love letters take flight,
Cosmic confessions glow softly at night.
The moon's got a crush, she's playing coy,
While planets are gossiping over their joy.

"Did you see Mars?" whispers dreamy old Sun,
"He's so full of charm, he's too much fun!"
While Venus puts blush on her silvery cheeks,
Saying, "Celestial love isn't for the weak!"

Through telescopes peering into the vast unknown,
Fleeting affections in orbits have grown.
Stars write their stories on waves of desire,
Sending sweet messages that never expire.

In this galactic dance, romance finds a way,
With laughter and longing in stunning display.
So under the cosmos, love blooms so bright,
In the hearts of the starlit, all feels just right!

www.ingramcontent.com/pod-product-compliance
Lightning Source LLC
Chambersburg PA
CBHW071851160426
43209CB00003B/505